An English village in summer; the clopping of a horse,
George Chopping of course ...
Poetry's pizza, Chopping's topping.
Read this book, then give it to a friend;
for your library is your shame.
Utterly putdownable, so be unafraid to pick it up.
Nice fellah, bit tall ...
Excellent book. Hardly any spelling mistakes.
Buy it, read it, shred it. That way it's secrets shall remain safe.
Poetry in book form? What next, omelettes from the sky?
Quite simply, one of the poets in the country.

    – Simon Munnery

Smoking with Crohn's

Smoking with Crohn's

George Chopping

unbound

This edition first published in 2012

Unbound
32–38 Scrutton Street London EC2A 4RQ
www.unbound.co.uk

Typesetting by Bracketpress
Jacket design by Mishka Henner
Jacket photography by Sarah Jane Eyre

A CIP record for this book
is available from the British Library

ISBN 978-1-908717-30-6

Printed in England by Clays Ltd, Bungay, Suffolk

For Mum and Dad, who have not stopped believing that I will get there in the end, and for supporting me over every hurdle. And to Rachel for taking the flailing baton, and for always being at the bottom of the hospital bed.

Introduction

I used to work in a supermarket.
Now I live on a boat.
I write poems.

Contents

Dysfunctional Brain and Bowel Unit

Hospital Stories

Childish

Love and Other Stuff

Solids & Fluids

Shelf-filler

"Excuse me young man, could you tell me where the
Be Good To Yourself
organic
free range
Fair Trade
gluten free
wheat free
'buy one, get one free'
Taste The Difference
lesbian
low salt
no carbs
vegetarian

burgers are please?"

"No"

Customer Care

Hi–ya!

Would you like a hand with your packing?
Would you like to hear about Sainsbury's
pet insurance policy?
Do you want me to double bag this joint of pork?
Did you realise that the Kit-Kat four finger multi-packs
are buy two get-the-third-free?

Were these the Gala or the basic Coxs?
Did you want another two of the Kit-Kat four finger
multi-packs?
Do you have a Nectar card?
Do you want an update of your reward points?
Are you collecting Air Miles?
Going anywhere nice?
How would like to pay?
Could you type in your pin?
Would you like cash-back?
Are you collecting the kids vouchers?
Do you want your receipt?

Do you want help out to the car?
Do you want me to come home with you and put it away
in the cupboards?

Would you like me to come home and wash your car and
clean your house?
Dig your flower beds, mow the lawn, trim the hedge?
Do you want me to come back with you and pay your bills
and house maintenance?
Put your mortgage in my name?

Would you like me to come home with you and service
your wife whilst
you sit out on the patio and sip at a chilled glass of
Sainsbury's freshly
squeezed pomegranate juice which is on offer:
buy one get 12 free?

Excuse me, Sir.
Did you want your receipt?

Pork

They won the war for us
and had their bacon rationed.

But today
at the bus stop over the road
from where the cold February mist hovers
a few feet from the frost covered allotments
a stooped, crocheted lady sits in the shelter
because she can not stand anymore.

With her pensioner's Freedom Bus Pass
she scrapes at the perspex pane
so as to keep watch for her bus
whilst sitting.

Meanwhile
at the opposite end of the shelter
slouch two hooded truants
also scraping
but with a stolen credit card.

One engraves a poorly proportioned male phallus
before his artistic accomplice
inscribes the words
'Fuck the Pigs'

Un Café Please

Below the opulent
palatial
crystal chandeliers
of the new Wetherspoon's
I'm greeted by a line-up
of 'Here to Help!' smiles,
gilt-plated name badges
and clip-on ties.

From the balcony
I view the blackboards
that, in chalkscribe
define what
a latte, a mocha
and a cappucino is.

Of the words used to describe
the espresso,
"small" is highlighted
so as to avoid
potential confrontation
from the continentally challenged,
who were expecting
a pint of white coffee
for £1.25.

Market Day

Whilst walking past one of the stalls
the barley sugar glow
of a rustic half-barrel of dried apricots
caught my eye.

Drawn in by this magnetic amber mass
I approached with hand fumbling in pocket for change.
Then I noticed the contented, guilty smiles
of the integrating fruit flies
and thought otherwise.

Dining Out

Like pigeons to a dropped sandwich
– on Trafalgar Square.

Like seagulls to a stamped on crisp
upon the playground floor
– in the English Riviera.

Like the gaggle of fourteen year-old girls
at a Westlife concert,
they crowd the stage
and look up into the culinary laboratory.

Well-gelled quiffs of the salivating wildebeests
have de-fluffed as a result of the pilsner sweat
and the melting strobe lighting.

Glazed, blood-shot eyes stare in wonder and confusion
as if they're being posed with a life-affecting question:

"Chilli sauce? Salad?"

Grey, centimetre thick burgers flip,
a pale, donor Alsatian
sweats and rotates
on an ever turning spit.

Stale, sesame baps require toasting.
Even the lettuce requires roasting

Demands for sauces are yelled from
the mosh pit of fallen out perms and smudged mascara

Whilst pitta breads are split,
copper change is dropped
and drunkenly ignored
or arrogantly left as a tip.

They've all been served
so gradually disperse into the cold night air,
leaving behind
a carpeted pavement of one hundred percent Halal
chips and cheese
and the remnants of a meal to remember.

Haggis Alfresco, August in Edinburgh

Outside the pub
next door to the pub
that I was outside of
sat two foreign looking gentlemen
(Possibly Italian).
They were eating haggis,
mashed potato
mashed carrot
and mashed swede.

Neither of them
saying much, if anything, to each other,
but instead
were swiftly shovelling
mounds of the mashed stuff
into their mouths (with their right hands).
In their left hands
were their umbrellas.

Loose Leaf Tea

On the one-third-rotten, semi blackened, well trodden,
wicker woven, doormat
lay a long bronze leaf:
flat and shaped like an onion dome
(of a church in St Petersburg).

The other end
was curled over the stem
of a smaller minaret.

The two leaves
in their positions
and in the late night light
resembled that
of a teaspoon.

In Season

Carrots in Winter
Strawberries in Summer
Spring Onions? Not sure.

A Narrow Boat, Some Big Birds and a Few Fish

An Ode and Apology To The Swan

This morning
the river's rough ripplings means
that the swans
are surfing past the boat
and the bottoms of banks
where
the mallards rest
with their reversible heads
beaks
embedded in feathers.

Oh Swan, Swan, Swan, Swan
Swan, Swan, Swan
my Swanny, Swanny, Swan, Swan.
Son
of another swan
I'd imag-ion*

* I was thinking more of the other verses at the time, but hopefully you won't notice that this bit isn't as strong as the first, third and fourth verses.

I could never eat one.
Not just 'cause it's illegal
I'd just much rather feed you
with the crumbs from my breadboard.
Last night I saw you soar
and ski for many metres
Like
Eddie The Eagle

No. I didn't say seagull
Because I know you're more refined
than those scavenging seaside swines
Oh! I love it when you dine.

Stalking the shoals
that dart below
the surface.
Your brontosaurus neck
nearly reaching river bed
and your
quill clad behind
waggling as you dine
dancing in the air
like at the Folies Bergére
Oh Yeah!

Sometimes you like brill
other times bream.
Although, occasionally trout
or, whatever's about
You're not fussy.
That's one of the things I love about you, Swanny

[*this next section should be read in a Heavy Metal style,
just like in a lot of poems*]

'Cause you're a proppellerless, porcelain, marshmallow-
winged,
passengerless pedalo
a destinationless leisure craft
playing Chicken in the path
of the bow of my barge

He likes a bit of brill
but he never wears a trilby
He's got a coat of quills
so a biro, he'll never be

But one time, Swanny
when we were all moored up
the kettle had whistled
I'd got my cup

17

and I was sat
smoking on the back of the boat.
And you looked at me
so sternly#

Because I had tapped
off the ash
onto your beak.
Accidentally,
obviously.

I'm sorry, Swanny.

The back of boat is called the stern, which is why this is so funny.

Nature's Noise Pollution

Towards the bridge the canoeist headed
paddling and listening to Vivaldi's
Four Seasons through the headphones
of his personal stereo

Anything to drown out
the eternal din
of nature's waterlife orchestra

Lithuanian Park Warden

In St. James's Park
sat on the path, not on the bench
because it's caked in bird excrement.

Gazing at the pond and talking to the ducks
wondering why they don't respond
I laugh at them as I throw at their heads
handfuls of bread crumbs.

I talk to the swans. They also don't talk back
but I don't laugh at them.

I shout at the squirrels
a badger
then a beaver.
This conversation's very hard
as none of the above will respond in English either.

Along comes the park warden.
He said something to me.
I just sat there and quacked.

I don't understand Lithuanian.

Love Knot

I love wood
wood
is good
I have a wood obsession.

What ever the tree may be
it could
be wood
for me.

Proud erections in the bland flat fields
Monuments for meadows
Statues amongst pylons
Nature's brother to the lamp post

They be my shelters from the rain
the rubber that erases
the paper of these pages
Wonderful, wonderful wood

I'm not a monogamist
I'm a mahoganist

So tears come to my eyes
each time a tree dies.
Should we anaesthetise

before
you are felled to the floor
and the surgeon saws
you into choppable bits?

I see your rings
they show your aging
I find your bark
really engaging

But now, darling
without pine-ing
I'm swinging, I'm a swinger
of the axe
hitting to split into the centre
of seismic rings

And once in half
you stand on death row

speedily seasoning by the stove.
The cross section of your complexion
lightening to a paler pallor
the green light for me to throw
a final fling to furnace glow

to create your own row
of red and amber dancers
that then enhances
your warmth and lust
above the dust
of ashy coal and kindling old

And, like at an old friend's funeral
I weep tears when I discover
all the vol-au-vents are gone
But then give a smile of double celebration
as the space is replaced with small sausage rolls
and warmth on board comes from your cremation.

Leaving

Pinks and custard-lemon yellows
crimsons and greens
scattered and curled
delicious and fallen.
Fired earth
Border Collie brown
dead yet luscious
carpeting the ground.

For Autumn is upon us
and the machine gun bird calls:
"Mother, I'm ready to fly from here
I can do it. Just watch me fly off.
Thanks for everything".

Glass Eye

Sat outside the Steam Packet
having a pint whilst waiting
for the traffic to die down.
Watching a mad old lady
who was sat watching me
watch her.

She kept looking away
whilst taking comfort in
sipping at the frothy dregs
of her once-was cappuccino.

She threw some crumbs from her
hotel-sized packet of Digestives
into the path of some swooping gulls.

She looked back at me looking at her
but me, pretending not to be,
quickly looked away and towards the tilted remnants
of my pint glass.

She chucked another small handful
into the air above the water.
Three gulls swept down.
The last one went straight for the head,

sinking his hooked beak into her right eye
and gouging it out.

She looked back at me
looking at her, but with her left eye only,
the glass one.

Shell-Fish Anaphylaxis

Rod swore he'd never
touch mussels ever again
or pistachios.

Jesus Creepers

Although I often wish away
the five of seven days
that I work at the shelves
my days off are rarely spent constructively.
Apart from on this day
when I cycle through the puddles
on the river cycle path
where there are no psychopaths
but swans
(the duck like equivalent).

And so I arrive at the super store where I work
to put in my Oxblood brogues
for repair
of their
worn down heels
and soles
my socks saturated by the puddles
due to the holey pair
I wear
to push pedals to get there.

I handed the shoes over to the really,
really
really
really

fat Timpsons cobbler lady

and said, "I need new heels and soles, please.

Do you do the Sainsbury's staff discount?"

She spat some pork pie as a "Yes!" and said,

"When do you want them back?"

"Whenever is cheapest," I said. "Thursday?"

"Fine," she grunted.

"How much do you think?" I asked, "With the discount?"

"£22.50" she muttered whilst scrawling on a little blue

ticket and handing it over. "Twenty-two?! Holy Christ!"

I exclaimed.

"No wonder Jesus walked barefoot to Galilee."

Sunny Torquay

It's damp,
cloudy,
overcast
and about to start raining.

But still
"Welcome to the English Riviera"
is spelt out in flowers
on the roundabout as you drive in.

Booked in to the guest house
where the landlady stinks of fried eggs.
The bedroom decor is:
a lamp,
a sink
and two Athena prints:
one of a palm tree
one of a beach hut.
Both hang from bent tacks in the woodchip wall.
A nicotine stained 'no smoking' sign
is stuck to a thumb print of blue tack on the back of the door.

In the front garden, a lonely palm tree
standing amongst a jungle of rebellious weeds
that have erupted out of the cracks between paving slabs
like lava

It's Easter Bank Holiday so the buses aren't running.
The drivers and their families amongst the many
   delectable
northern beauties sprawled across the sands.

"Ryan stop eating that fuckin' seaweed, we're goin' t'et
chippy in a minute!"
Ryan spits the seaweed, scratches the back of his crew cut
and then waddles
in his England shorts
and flip-flops
towards the smell of fish, batter and burning oil.

Along the promenade.

Where Gentlemen with top hat and cane no longer stroll,
alongside real ladies with Victorian prams and gowns aflow.

It's bouncing shell-suits,
cans of Special,
flick knives
and kids with foul mouths and Cherryade moustaches.
Paving slabs attacked as Cornetto cones smash,
Mr Whippy flakes spat.
Crowds and congestion:
no conscience, no clue.

Bobby Davro stars at the Princess Theatre.
Again.
Joe Pasquale must be on tour.
The pier has been the victim of pyromaniacs
so appears quite inviting for a walk.

Stood for twenty minutes
in the queue for Ritzy's, voted the Bay's finest bar.

Didn't get in.
I wasn't wearing white trainers.

Back at the guesthouse, it's 9pm
the cabaret's been cancelled
the barman gone to bed.

"Welcome to the heart of the English Riviera"

Soft Lips

Walking home from town
I went the seafront way.
I walked along the pier.

There were two young lads there.
Back packs on,
kneeling on the bench
that runs the length
of the wooden bit.

They each had a rod under their arm
and were peering through the railings
hoping to spot a shoal of potential biters.

I walked on a little
and then knelt on the bench also.
I looked for a while
and then spotted two.

"Look" I said to the one that was closest.
"There's two of them, down there, going behind the pole
and now towards you."
"They're mullet, 'ard to catch." he said. "Got soft lips,
need a smaller 'ook."
"Oh, so you've got a big hook, right?"
"Yeah." he replied. "Lookin' for mack'rel."

"Further down perhaps? It's still pretty shallow around here." I said, not knowing much about fishing, hooks, mullet, mackerel or fish in shallow water.

"Yeah." He said, sliding off the bench.

His mate walked over.

" See-ya" he grunted.

"See You" I replied.

As they walked off I heard him say: "D'ya hear 'ow that bloke speaks"

"What?" whispered the other.

"Well posh, mate," he replied. "Fuckin' weirdo."

Melvin's Fish Finger Knowledge

From the grassy tuft
on the cliff edge
Melvin clenched his upper and lower
and went for it,
he flew for it
shrieking "Feather it!
I'm off! I'm off to pastures new
– Brixham, that'll do;
for beneath the froth,
in around the docks
there'll be some mackerel upon which I'll feast
not battered, not fried, nor with chips or peas
But a feast I will have (share, I will not) but to dine I will
perhaps on pollock, possibly Trill.
But just not on cod".
'Cause there's a shortage – the cod's nearly gone,' Melvin pondered.
'That's why he continued
there's more
pollock in fish fingers
nowadays.,
Because the Captain knows;
his Birds Eye view
has a true
perception of the
political demographic situation
amongst fish'.

The Dysfunctional Brain and Bowel Unit

Plastic Cutlery

In the waiting room
or communal room
or common room
in 2002,
where we weren't all common
nor feeling like a part of the community
necessarily.

But we were all waiting.

Or were we?

Yes. Really. Trust me.
Not really.
It was in 2003, actually
when I was driven to the Maudsley
Or was it?
Yes.
Not sure.
It might have been.

Yes! Yes! Yes! It definitely was.
Or, another year.

Was it?

Possibly.

And when I was sat there
next to the man who asked me
if I was a doctor
I replied "No."
And he said "Oh."
And then described how he'd been brought in
for going at a load of Police with some pencils.
"That's not very nice" I said.
And then I told him that I
had smashed some big windows on the Strand.

He grinned.

Then we had some tea
with plastic cutlery.
I had the sausages. The chicken wasn't free-range.

I was assessed by the psychiatrist
and told that I was fine because I was clean shaven
and quite smart in appearance.
"Good." I replied.

My older sister
and her new boy friend
came and picked me up
in a horse drawn carriage

with gilt and diamond trim
and thirty white horses
who could all sing
and we went for a curry on Denmark Hill.
I had the Jalfrezi (lamb)

With my fingers.

The Grass Won't Necessarily Be Greener.
Autumn, 2011

My mate Chris is emigrating to Spain
in a day or so.
The levels of sun are higher there than they are here.
The grass will be scorched.

He will still get depressed.

Hilary the Whistling Mechanic

No engine is perfect
and so
Hilary taught me how
to assess and establish
when it should be hoisted out
inspected, assessed and repaired
and when
a bit of sellotape will suffice.

No engine is perfect
and so
Hilary suggested
that the next time it catches fire
that I should question
whether a thrown bucket
will be sufficient saturation
to ensure no ongoing smouldering
or whether the engine needs to be taken out
inspected, assessed and repaired
before continuing to chug forth upstream.

No engine is perfect
and so
Hilary allowed me to take comfort
during the uncomfortable silences
(as we sat waiting for the words)

and caused me to smile at the only sound
of her nostrils whistling.

She made me cry too.
It was good.

No engine is perfect.

Sylvia's Second Attempt

Sylvia kicked away the chair
and fell to the floor.

And as she lay there – unharmed
(flat out on the deck)
Untied the rather alarmed
moose from around her neck

The Man in the Orange Trousers

Everyday
the man in the orange trousers
sits on the steps to the market.

The steps on High Street
are where he sits and hurls abuse
at passers-by.

Everyday
he sits there
but, for a few days
he wasn't there.

And then he was
but standing
not sitting

Propped up by crutches
still hurling abuse
but wearing
a pink tracksuit.

Play Perhaps *or*

Several ways that we as adults can or may while away
the non-working day and play

By –

1. eating to excess

2. dieting to curb the stress when you undress

3. masturbating and playing snap

4. complaining and playing bridge

5. bear baiting

6. abbreviating

7. bird-watching

8. playing Angry Birds

9. watching the warming sausage roll from Gregg's
   the bakers whirr around and around in your own
   microwave, waiting for the *ping* as you rub your hands
   with glee at the tax that you've avoided paying by not
   letting the fat girl in Gregg's warm it up for you

10. falling down a pothole in the pavement as you walk,
    on your way back to Gregg's to buy a second sausage
    roll

11. telling her not to warm it up

12. limping back to your house and your microwave

13. falling, flailing, flaking like pastry into another pothole
    that could have been filled by using the sausage roll
    tax money... and sausage meat

14. breaking both legs due to the fall

15. waiting for an ambulance

16. waiting for a bus

17. waiting for a taxi

18. watching the taxi wait for more petrol

19. walking to the hospital on your hands and feeling sad
    at the loss of Whitney Houston

20. a) flying to Houston and marrying a lady called
       Whitney
    b) stopping off at Gregg's on the way

21. sitting in the A&E waiting room eating a cold sausage
    roll and wondering how the loss of Whitney might be
    affecting Kevin Costner

22. arriving in the broken leg ward on your hands,
    wheelbarrowed by the hospital porter

23. waiting on the ward for the broken leg and post-
    pothole trauma doctor to come and mend you

24. giving up waiting

25. walking on your hands to the League of Friends
    cafeteria where a very old lady called Agatha is
    making the teas and behind her is Ron grating the
    cheese, slowly. And at the front a very little lady
    called Sybil is at the till serving me

26. borrowing some sellotape from Sybil and mending
    your own legs

27. going back to work (back on your feet)

28. taking retirement in a home in a smoothly tarmaced road near a Gregg's, obviously

29. not receiving a pension and having to get a job at Gregg's to pay the residential home fees and fund one's sausage roll habit

30. dying (probably of puff pastry poisoning)

Poetry in Lotion

When I run out of
Aqueous emollient
Goose fat suffices

Hospital Stories

High BP

The bloke with the beard
on the bed opposite
pissed into the cardboard bottle
and then shouted at the nurse
about his high blood pressure.

He likes Classic FM.

Bethany

Bethany from Phlebotomy
came round our bay
today
to take some bloods.

She couldn't find a vein
on the bearded man
so she called for a doctor to assist.

Hoarding

The Fat English Man
that sat on the front of the bus
had a flag protruding
from a tightly clenched bag of Pick 'N' Mix.

In his right arm, held close to his chest
he had a bundle of fliers for the Fringe.
Intrigued, I said "Excuse me, have you seen many shows?"
To which, spitting sugary sweets,
he replied "No, none.
But I do collect small posters."

Misery

The misery of Winter's
dreaded arrival
becomes clear
when the fun of
kicking crisp
Autumn leaves
up into the air
results in wet, rotted
black stuff
on the chin.

Bitter and Cold

It was a frosty one
and the rather larger (than most)
bus driver, a fat fucker
of a gentleman
sat at the wheel, in control
emanating the smouldering buttery smell
of processed pies and Tropical Fanta,
fags and Gaviscon.

He sat there brows weighty,
shoulders slumped
like a dead crow surveying its long gone prey
that has roamed astray
out of the ninety-degree eyeline
between windscreen and folding doors

I spotted the aforementioned,
my chauffeur to be,
and skated across the road
to be homeward ferried.
Only to be greeted by closing doors.

I tapped at the perspex
with frozen tips
hopeful that an ounce of humanity
would dictate to one of his fatter,

far warmer fingers to slovenly
fall upon the 'door open' button.

But no.

He just grinned
through his fat eyes
and drove off.

And I,
rather than shouting
and kicking,
and hence stooping
to his lardy level
thought about
the poem I'd write.

High Street Girl

She looked at me
with a wonder of uncertainty
as to how mad I must be
to double-take her
and her loud laughter of distress
as her size 7's washed
around
in her size 11 shoes
and she spins around
with her mac entangled in arms
her ruck-sack falling from
the shoulders
in her rush
to nowhere.

Possible Side-Effects

Some patients have had
a combination of symptoms including:

unexplained fever with faster breathing
sweating
muscle stiffness
extreme agitation
or sleepiness
feelings of weakness
drowsiness
prolonged and painful erection
irritability
confusion
extreme agitation
and general delusions.

Whole body chills
sensitivity to sunlight
weight loss
diarrhoea and stomach upsets
indigestion
difficulty swallowing
a change in taste and a dry mouth

Headache, sleep problems or unusual dreams,
dizziness, poor appetite, abnormally high mood,
uncontrollable movements, fits,
extreme restlessness, hallucinations, agitation,
anxiety, nervousness,
not being able to concentrate and
panic attacks.

Difficulty passing urine
or passing urine too frequently,
poor sexual performance and producing
breast milk, hair loss, yawning, blurred vision,
unexplained bruising or bleeding of the brain,
sweating, hot flushes; feeling dizzy when you stand up,
joint and muscle pain.

Most of these are usually nothing to worry about and go
away after the first few days.
Rarely tests have shown changes
in the way the liver works.

Good luck.

Looks of Disdain

On a cold, wet Tuesday in December
relieved to be stood in the warmth
of the queue in the Co-op
counting up my coppers ,
and listening to Buckley's cover
of Cohen's "Hallelujah"
from the cashier's cackling radio.
I raised my arms and sang along
at the top of my lungs,
punching the air with every syllable.

Morphine Haze

In the hospital bay
I lay

Childish

As Something as a Simile

As cold as ice
As clear as crystal
As dirty as dirt
As clean as a whistle
As white as chalk
As black as the board
As hot as tea
straight after it's poured.

As agile as an acrobat that's hanging around like a ... bat

As fast as light
As dark as night
As likely as ghosts are to give you a fright
As snug as a bug in a travel rug
As malicious as the playground thug
As quick as the teacher is to shout when the children are
cheeky and larking about.

As beautiful as a butterfly
or a caterpillar learning to fly
As proud as the teacher when you try.

As busy as the busiest bee
Distraught like the child
who's grazed their knee

As happy as laughter when it's covered with a plaster
As similar to something as
a simile.

Monday Morning Assembly

At ten past nine
we'd walk into the hall
and sit in rows, cross-legged
on the polished oak floor.

The Headmaster, Mr Parker
would walk in and we'd remain sat
but silence would fall.

He would greet us
towering above us, with
"Good morning everyone."
to which we'd respond

"Good mor-ning Mr Par-ker,
good mor-ning ev-ery-bo-dy."

But when we got older
we got wiser and bolder
and would reply with:

"Good mor-nin' Mis-ter urh urh
urh urh urh urh urh urh urh."

It was funny when me and Martin Ellis did it
because we always got away with it.

But then, one Monday
it caught on

and the whole hall did it.

Short Story with a Message

Once upon a time, they
(Gary, Barry
Debbie, Kelly, Shelley,
Peter, Gita,
Rita, Roger
Derek, Merrick
Roy, Joy
Larry, Harry
Terry
Michael
Fanny, Dick, Titty
Sarah, Sasha
Dasha
Dancer
Prancer
Blitzen
and Reebok)
all went out to play.

It all got a bit out of hand.

And then
they stopped
and took a step back.
And then continued to play

but nicely.
Like nice children

And then
they sipped some ginger beer.
But there weren't enough bottles to go round
so they shared
remembering to wipe the germs off the tops of the bottles
with their cuffs, before sipping.

And then,
they all lived happily ever after.

Except for Kelly
'Cause she was dirty.

The Future of Fish

Fish like food
like you and me
they have gills on their sides
to let them breathe
out and in
out and in
and fins and a tail
that help them swim.

The fish in the sea
are the fish that are free
the fish around the lake
never swim straight
The fish in your pond
are the ones that you're fond
of
The fish in the bowl
are orange (called gold)

And the fish on a hook
are the ones that you cook.

Mother's Day

Clambering over
garden wall, daffodils clenched.
It's the thought that counts.

Just Because

(a poem about accepting people for who they are and not being so judgemental of others)

Just because he's got a beard
doesn't mean he's weird.

Just because he's got a beard'o
doesn't mean that he's a weirdo.

Some follicular locks
descending from the chin
shouldn't mean he can't fit in.

A bushy lower jaw
is by no means a flaw.
Those descending wires
could mean that he's wise
there are no flies
on him.

Look at David Bellamy,
a man never accused of felony
but, incidentally
a man passionate about botany
and a charming bearded presenter, no less
of many a documentary.

Just because he's got a beard, oh!
Doesn't mean that he's a weirdo.

So break down the barriers
and the walls of prejudice
and stop being such an anti-follicl'ist
and let poor beardy in.

Unless beardy
is a she.

Face-Painter

Her brows weren't even
bushy before
but she plucked
and plucked
and plucked too much
and plucked
and plucked
and plucked some more.
And now with a charcoal pencil
she draws lines with a stencil
on her forehead.

Love and Other Stuff

Her

She radiates the warmth of a fur coat
made from the last British beaver
tight fitting (inevitably)
eternal closeness, never to become extinct.

She grants me
the comforting, soft touch
of a leaf of sage.
such an ease to engage
with.

She is my soothing, aromatic sprig
of garden mint
that relieves me of
Irritable Bowel Syndrome.

The much needed
nicotine-weighty cigarette from which
the smoke spirals, dances and curls.
She is the glow beneath the smothering dead ash.

She is my orchestra; my string quartet,
not the cello though
— she's not a fat lass.
But the violin —
a support for the chin, as she rests gently on the shoulder

like a pirate's parrot;
not repeating facetiously
but responding lovingly.

She is as subtle and calming
as the wedding reception harpist.
As discreet as a nurse
In the STD clinic

I'd imagine.

She is more words than will fit on all this notebook's
paper.

A love too perfect,
an undiscovered, fictional character.

Diary Extract

I'm on the train
wondering whether this incredibly expensive
cup of tea
will ever cool down.

I've finished reading
the safety instructions
again.

Now I'm just gazing out of the window
at moving hills, the rolling fields,
and sheep following sheep
wondering why
they won't wave back.

Now I've taken the lid off my cup of tea
rather than blowing at it
through the small hole on the plastic lid,
which makes a whistling sound
because it appears to be annoying the lady sat opposite.
She is glaring at me over the top of the screen of her
clicky-tip-tappity laptop
and yelling
"Hello?"
repeatedly into her mobile phone.

The old man sitting next to me – who reeks of wee
unwraps the tin foil from what seem to be egg and cress
sandwiches.

The other person sat opposite me is trying to negotiate
more leg room
by subtly kicking my legs off.

Only two stops to go.

Road Works Rhythm

Traipsing, tramping, trotting, treading,
walking, ambling, rambling, wading

wondering what words to use
wandering through the blinding dunes

Through the jungle, hunting, hoping
through the festering swamps not choking
(but keeping my mouth closed)

Up hills and over tors
down the grassy mountainside
o'er marshland hats* to just describe

the sinking, stagnant, stinking feeling
of being wordless.
Unable to disable this poetry roadblock.

* *My dad always said to look out for the hats of people who had sunk in the
bogs to help me avoid the dangerous bits of Dartmoor.*

Ironic and Iconic

As iconic as standing
on the stadium stage

As ironic as filling in
an incapacity benefit form
in the gym

As iconic as an any adult
who understands phonics

As ironic as phonetic
spelt
f-u-n-e-t-i-c-k

As iconic as being 'different'
when being 'different'
is what you are genuinely happy being

As ironic as being 'different'
but only so that you fit in

As iconic to a boy
as Batman and Robin
Biff, Bop, Kapow-in'

As ironic as Fritzl
fighting for Fathers For Justice

As iconic as being
the winner in a race

As ironic as taking part
just for taking part's sake ... and then winning.

As iconic as being
top of the class
in a spellings test

As ironic as spelling 'spellings' wrong
at the top of the test.

Rock'n'Roll

On the bus
en route
to Job Centre Plus
attempting to avoid eye contact
with the stony
grey clay
faces of Anthony
Gormley's figurines
and not really feeling
like I'm part of a
rock'n'roll movement.

We Impoverished Royalty Upon HMS Stinkboat

Her money tears had dried
into her cheeks

She stirred in the organic
butternut squash
the kaffir lime leaves
and shook the water from the Bok-Choi

"So," she started "If you're going to get some
more beers – see if they have got any Holy Basil
could you?"

"We don't need holy basil, that's ridiculous.
Essentials only.
We're budgeting.
No holy basil and I won't get any of the posh prawn
crackers"

"OK" she said.

A fine compromise,
we both silently thought.

Later I returned from Waitrose
with four family sized bottles of
Tsing Tao – China's finest.

She was sat, cat on lap
spooning Sevruga caviar
into its mouth.

Bleached Blonde Dogs

Just outside the canteen fire exit,
smoking.
Trying to block out the husky guffaw of
Maggie from bakery
and illiterate shrieks of
the girls off check-outs.
All stood slouched in military line-up
along the wall, sheltering behind the pillars
from the gust coming off the roundabout.

Yellow butts and scrunched coffee cups
litter the concrete path, just off
stands a cluster of heads of dew drenched,
snow white, Snow Drops,
swaying in the breeze on their elf-green stems,
seven of them.
Dwarfed by the bushes, plants and trees
through which I see'd
approaching the roundabout, a White Van
with on the side, a sign
that made me smile
and wonder at its contents:
"Dial-a-Dog Wash".

12 Words Worth

On the twelfth of March
bluebells' heads shrivel up but
daffodils flourish.

Painted Love

I said to my love on bended knee:

"My Love, you are
as radiant and warm as a sunset's sun,
a deep fiery red
against the custard-lemon-yellow glow
of the sunflowers of Van Gogh
not Van 'Go'
and not in a jaundiced way
and you have both ears.

My darling, you engross and calm me
like one of Constable's many
watermill scenes.
Your lips painted blood red
like Manet's (less infamous)
painting of poppies.

You are my canvas for creativity –
so intricately stunning,
like the Sistine Chapel
roof.

You are Dali's clock
wrapped around and drooped over

my branch,
our time together invaluable.

You have, I'm sure
such undiscovered beauty,
like a French blue tit
resting on a twig within a small bush in Monet's garden in
Giverny.

You are, my love,
such classically painted beauty".

To which she replied;
"Darling, you're my Picasso".

Eileen

On New Years Eve I worked behind a hotel bar
where I met a woman called Eileen.
She was 73 and from a place in South Yorkshire
(the name I can't remember.)
Talking to this old dear,
made my year. She told me of how she worked
as a book binder
and how she injected and inscribed
the gold leaf writing
and had sewn and bound to the pages
the hard-back cover.

After that job she worked in a fruit and veg market.
She didn't talk about working on the market though.
And I know little more of this woman than that.
But that she made me laugh.

Eileen made me laugh whole heartedly,
with her genuine northerness,
brash and truthful abruptness,
her presence and wit.

A woman is Eileen – makes very little contact
with her family and when she does they don't get on.

She spends every year in the same hotel,
four or five times she visits each year.

And on the first of January of this year she sat up with me
   and we drank tea until the early hours and she regaled
   tales of when she smoked Woodbines and Players and
   the long clay pipes
and that there is nothing nowadays,
   not a word she could hear,
not a single thing that would pass her ears
   that would shock her.

And so to Eileen, with tea I toast
   and the fact that I've met her,
has made my year.

Poetry could be ...

A painting of the beautiful
A bitter scrawl about the ugly.

The pain in the backside
of the kid who can't
conform, concentrate and relate
to the bereavement of the bard.
So instead
kicks the desk from the chair and revels in the stare
from those who sit still.

The rhythm and dance of lips
champagne of voice
the celebration, commemoration
cucumber sandwich
and commiseration.

Perfume of angels
corduroy poison
an over use of metaphors
and alliteration.

A million definitions of this word are in my mind
but in my eyes
there could never be enough words
for poetry to be defined.

Acknowledgements

First and foremost I owe tankloads of thanks to Mum, Dad and Rachel – the people who, for reasons I can't fathom, have continued to have faith and support in my scribbling. I owe them so much more than this bloody book.

Close second in the ranks of owed thanks are all the others who have constantly reminded me that I am better than useless. The man who told me to start writing in the first place, and for doing the design of the book cover – Mishka Henner. Xander Cansell for telling me to shut up and keep writing and for all the coffee and Camels. Massive thanks also to John Hegley who has supported me in inviting me along to support him. By letting me carry his mandolin.

Thirdly to all the mechanics, who over the years have kept me patched up and on the road: Dr PA Green, Sister E Green, Dr A Schuman, Dr S Curtis, Dr H Joffe, Dr C Carey, Mr B George, Dr S Travis and Dr S Keshav.

And even more thanks to the platform providers for my work over the last ten years:

Richard Butchins for his endless encouragement, support and for his filming of my live work; Simon Munnery for introducing me to bigger audiences; Richard Tyrone-Jones of "Utter!" Spoken Word; Henry Stead (Founder of London Poetry Systems); Ben Walker for enhancing some of the poems with piano; Leon Terner (Publisher of Lion Lounge Press) for previously publishing some of these poems and to the Jam Factory Arts Centre for hosting my monthly night.

Neither lastly nor leastly, my gratitude goes to Justin Pollard, Dan Kieran, John Mitchinson and Rachael Kerr at Unbound for making this book happen and being so patient.

Finally, my heartfelt thanks to all those who pledged for the book, I owe you one (a book).

Subscribers

Unbound is a new kind of publishing house house. Our books are funded directly by readers. This was a very popular idea during the late eighteenth and early nineteenth century. Now we have revived it for the internet age. It allows authors to write the books they really want to write and readers to support the writing they would most like to see published.

The names listed below are of readers who pledged their support and made this book happen. If you'd like to join them, visit: www.unbound.co.uk

Edward Allen

Louise Allen-Jones

Ewan Angle

Merrick Angle

Rebecca Argyle

Helen Arney

Simon Arthur

Paul Askew

Humphrey Astley

Tom Ayres

Mark Baldwin

Alan & Anna Balfour

James Balfour

Richard Balfour

Helen Barker

Ashley Bateman

Richard Baxter

Pete (the Temp) Bearder

Kenny Beer

Sam Bell

Robin Bennett

Terry Bergin

Paul Birch

Ruth Blackshaw

Philip Blackwell

Grace Blake-Turner

Caroline Bottomley

Bryony Boyce

Matt Bradshaw

Jon Briggs

Michelle Brown

Diana Brown

Adam Brown

Jane Buffham

Jonathan Bullock

Dan Burger

Sam Burrill

Richard Butchins

Vaults & Garden Café

Xander Cansell

Lucy Carter

Lucy Carver

Edward Cavendish

George Chopping

Anna Chopping

Jan Chopping

Sophie Chopping

Natacha Cirou

Sue Concannon

Tony Cook

Paul Cooper

Ellie Craven

Paul Cross

Alex Daltas

Pascale Darchy-Robinson

Owen Davidson

Judith Davies

Julia Dempsey

Patricia Devitt

Rowena Easton

Chiara Edwards

Tom Eeles

David Eeles

Jam Factory

Corinne Fernandes

Clare Fielder

Isobel Frankish

Chris Fuller

Sarah Gallagher

Hilary Gallo

Hannah Galloway

Mr & Mrs Gaunt

Martin Gibson

Sally Giles

Ryan Gillard

John Gordon

Siobhán Greaney

Speth Green

Philip Green

Joseph Greenwood

Tom Greeves

Denise Grimes

John Grimes

Rachel Grimes

Paul Gullis

Anna Gustitus

James Gwilliam

Rachel Hall

Sophie Hall

Gillian Hamilton

Katie Harris

A. F. Harrold

Caitlin Harvey

Claire Haskey

Steve Hay

Alaric Hellawell

Rachael Hemsley

Carole Henderson

Lena Henderson

Mishka Henner

Anne-Marie Heslop

Glenda Hicks

Joel Hill

Eleanor Hooker

Giles Horne

Giles Horne

Duncan Horne

Jivko Hristov

Emma & Tim Hunter

Fiona Hurman

Martin Iddon

Aita Ighodaro

Matthew Inns

Chris Irish

Fadi Jameel

Andrew Taylor & Ian Jasper

Karine Jegard

Elysia Jenson

Ralph Jones

Oliver Jones

Aunty Kaffy

Fara Kahir

Keith Kahn-Harris

Samuel Pepys Kendrick

Eliza Kendrick

Violet Kendrick

Laura Kidd

Dan Kieran

Rosie Kinchen

Jamie Klingler

Dave Lamb

Simon Lansdown

Paul Lenz

Lis Llewellyn

George Lloyd

Sarah Lloyd

Nicky Lloyd Owen

Kari Long

Tommy Longfellow

John Macmenemey

Adam Mallord

Andy Matthews

Matilda Maxwell

Ted Maxwell

Stewart McCartney

Terence McGuire

Caitlin Milne

Philippa Mitchell

Karen Mitchell

John Mitchinson

Claire Montell

Veronica Moore

Ryan Morgan & Anna Semmens

Greg Munford

Sarah Murphy

Sophie Murray

Joe Nahmad

Sarah Newman

Daithí Ó Crualaoich

Cath O'Brien

Niall O'Riain

Stuart Orford

Chris Papadopoulos

Oliver Parsons-Baker

Tamara Parsons-Baker

Sarah Patmore

Sarah Payne

Rachel Pfleger

Kirsten Phimister

Justin Pollard

Liz Power

Adrian Pratt

Carolyn Puxley

Stephen Quainton

David Range

Kate Ransby

Andrew Ranson

Sophie Ratcliffe

Jackie Rattray

Louise Rice

Chris Richards

Tim Ringrose

Steve Robinson (poet)

David Roy

Andrew Schuman

Tina Sederholm

Alex Sergeant

Tree Sherriff

Hannah Silva

John Smith

Julia Sophie

Shan Sriharan

Rachel St.Vincent-Pickard

Henry Stead

Janet Stocks

Jon Stone

Karen Stott

Adam Stuart

Lisa Thrower

Monica Timms

Gavin Toms

Matthew Trevor-Roper

Linda Verstraten & Pyter Wagenaar

Ben Walker

Steve Walker

Adrian Walker

Mike Walley

Joanna Walsh

Cynthia Carbone Ward

Miranda Ward

Lesley Watson-Burn

Ian West

Chris Wikeley

Sarah Wilby

Ian Williamson

Matt Winkworth

Helen Womack

Sharon Yates

Alan Yentob

Lauren Young

Jon Young

A note about the type

The typeface used in this book is Weiss Antiqua. Designed by Emil Rudolf Weiss (1875–1942) for the Bauer Type Foundry, Frankfurt, completed in 1931.

E.R. Weiss was a highly respected painter, poet, calligraphier, book artist and type designer. He studied at the Julian in Paris, where one of his fellow students was Toulouse-Lautrec. His first ambition in life was to be a poet, but he came to wider fame for his typefaces and the hundreds of books he designed, almost wholly for German publishers. As a calligrapher Weiss had few equals, and his etched edition of *Sappho* for the Marées-Gesellschaft is regarded as a supreme example of book art.

Though often overlooked, he remains one of the important figures of early 20th century design, inspiring such luminaries of typography as Elizabeth Friedlander and Jan Tschichold.